DATE DUE

FEB 21 2004		
MAR 13 2004		
AUG 11 2004		
DEC 04 2004		
11/23		

DEMCO 38-297

LIFE CYCLES
Ducks

by Melanie Mitchell

first step nonfiction

Lerner Publications Company · Minneapolis

Look at the **duck**.

There are many kinds
of ducks.

3

A duck is a bird, like a chicken or an **owl**.

How does a duck grow?

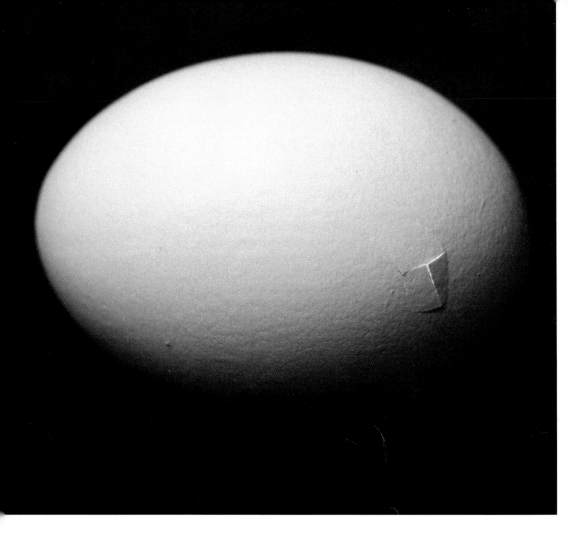

A duck starts as an egg.

The eggs are in a nest.

A mother duck keeps
the eggs warm.

One day, the eggs **hatch**.

Baby ducks are called
ducklings.

Ducklings stay with their mother.

The ducklings use their **webbed feet** to swim.

They learn to find food.

The ducklings grow bigger.

Young ducks learn to fly.

The young ducks fly to
a warm home.

It is fun to watch a
duck grow.

Parts of a Duck

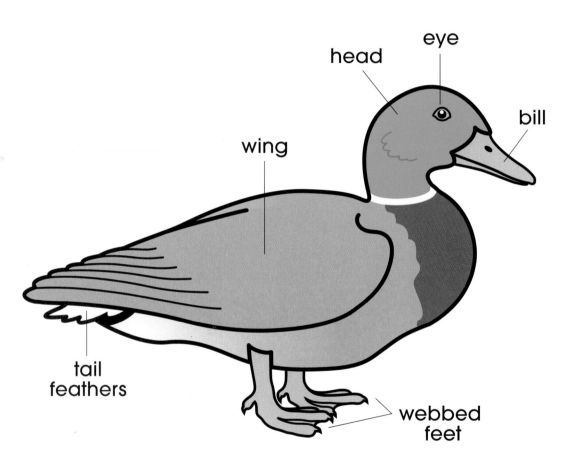

head

eye

bill

wing

tail
feathers

webbed
feet

Adult Ducks

There are many kinds and sizes of adult ducks. All ducks have the same basic body parts. They have webbed feet to help them swim. They also have wings for flying. Ducks have a mouth called a bill.

Many ducks migrate, or move, to warm places in the winter. In the spring, these ducks return to their homes. The ducks will then get ready to lay eggs and begin the duck life cycle again.

Duck Fun Facts

 Male ducks are the ones with the bright feathers. A female duck has dull feathers so she can hide better.

 A duck's feet cannot feel the cold. The feet do not have nerves.

 A duck's feathers are waterproof. Ducks have a special oil that coats their feathers to keep out the water.

Ducks can be found everywhere except Antarctica. It is too cold for them there.

 Female ducks quack louder than male ducks.

 A group of ducks is called a flock. When a bunch of ducks are swimming together, we say they are "rafting."

Glossary

 duck – a water bird with a bill and webbed feet

 ducklings – young ducks

 hatch – to come out of an egg

 owl – a bird with a large head and large eyes

 webbed feet – feet with skin between the toes

Index

The photographs in this book are reproduced through the courtesy of : © Lydia G. Parker, front cover, pp. 8, 17; © Allen Blake Sheldon, pp. 2, 3 (top left), 7, 11, 22 (top); © Rob Curtis, pp. 3 (top right, bottom left, bottom right), 13, 14, 15, 16; © Connie Toops, pp. 4, 22 (second from bottom); © Gay Bumgarner/Visuals Unlimited, p. 5; © Robert Pickett/CORBIS, p. 6; © William J. Weber/Visuals Unlimited, pp. 10, 22 (second from top); © Maslowski/Visuals Unlimited, pp. 9, 22 (middle); © Jane McAlonan/Visuals Unlimited, pp. 12, 22 (bottom). Illustration p. 18 by Laura Westlund.

Lerner Publications Company
A division of Lerner Publishing Group
241 First Avenue North
Minneapolis, MN 55401 USA

Website address: www.lernerbooks.com

Library of Congress Cataloging-in-Publication Data

Mitchell, Melanie S.
    Ducks / by Melanie Mitchell.
        p.   cm. — (First step nonfiction) (Life cycles)
    Summary: A basic overview of the life cycle of a duck and the behavior of ducklings as they grow.
    ISBN: 0–8225–4602–7 (lib. bdg. : alk. paper)
    1. Ducks—Life cycles—Juvenile literature. [1. Ducks. 2. Animals—Infancy.] I. Title.
II. Series.
QL696.A52 M55   2003
598.4'1—dc21   2002003283

Manufactured in the United States of America
1 2 3 4 5 6 – JR – 08 07 06 05 04 03